Fun with Coquinas
Tiny Hidden Treasures

Laura Pastuszek

Published by Writesville Publishing, Sarasota, FL

Printed in the United States of America

ISBN-13: 978-1-7321894-0-9

IN MEMORY OF MY MOTHER

A woman of faith, who exuded amazing fortitude, lived with great compassion for others, gave steadfast love, had a passion to write and paint, and infused me with incredible curiosity and inspiration for life!

CONTENTS

Fun with Coquinas: Tiny Hidden Treasures

Fun with Coquinas
Tiny Hidden Treasures

Photographs and text by Laura Pastuszek

Fun Facts about Coquinas

The tiny clams are found on many warm water beaches around the world. Some of those countries are the United States, France, England, Mexico and Western Australia. They have different names depending on where they are located. In the United States, among some of the places they have been found are in California, Florida, Georgia, Maryland, New York, North Carolina, South Carolina, Texas and Virginia.

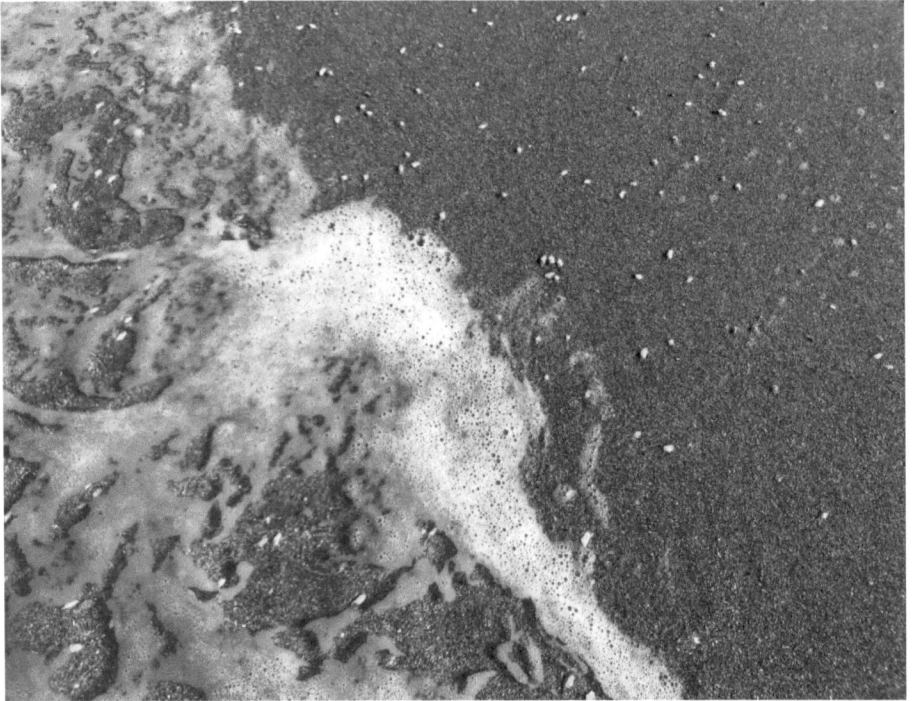

Coquinas are bivalve Mollusks and algae filter-feeders. They eat the "nutrients" of the sea. They are important for the health of the beach and an important part of the food chain.

Ghost crabs, sea snails, fish and seabirds eat the tiny clams along the water's edge within the tidal zone.

Most Coquinas are about the size of a dime when alive and closed. They are about the size of a nickel when no longer living and opened up.

The tides and waves help move the Coquinas up and down the beaches. These clams burrow themselves in the sand with their muscular foot. When it is time to migrate, the waves are very useful in carrying them along in the water.

It takes patience to spot Coquinas in the sand. Look for the brightly colored ones or they may go unnoticed. They come in light and darker hues of yellow, blue, red, purple, orange, and of course white. Many tiny clams have special patterns like the reddish orange one.

Coquinas also have special rings and patterns. The rings and patterns show rates of growth. Scientists have done studies to understand why and how these tiny clam shells get their rings, patterns and colors. The many colors in this one species of bivalves may protect them from the shorebird predators.

Fun Creative Writing Ideas with Coquinas

Nature is fun to see. It can be very inspiring. Sometimes it can be a tool to help with creativity and to write. Reading facts, asking questions, observing details and carefully writing about nature can be enough to make the words into a poem.

Small Hidden Treasure

I live at the sea,
sharing my other half with glee,
it's so special to be me.

My house is in a good place
although for me, birds do chase,
so digging in the earth, is at a quick pace.

With my foot, I slip down into the sand
to a fine land,
where I drink, eat and feel grand.

Rainbows of the Sea

The beauty way up high leads me to look below.
Like the colors of the rainbow, I find you
in the sand.
You spread out your tiny wings
to paint the
amazing land.

Fun Projects with Coquinas

There are an abundance of these nonliving shells found around the world. Although called by different names in different places, they all can be used to make beautiful arts and crafts. Here are just a few creative ideas. They make great souvenirs and reminders of wonderful beach memories.

MAKE DESIGNS

MAKE DECORATIONS

Layer different colors of Coquinas into an empty clear container.

MAKE ORNAMENTS

Craft stores sell empty clear plastic bulbs. Remove the top and carefully place the shells one at a time into the bulb.

MAKE SPECIAL CARDS

Make your design in the sand or on a card and take a picture. Print the picture and glue to an empty piece of folded cardboard.

3D ARTWORK

Use liquid glue and apply the Coquinas to the paper.

Fun with Coquina Games

Guess the word?

Collect Coquinas and use them to spell out words on the beach.

Match

Collect Coquinas and sort them according to different attributes. See how many categories can be made based on sizes, colors, and patterns.

Count how many Coquinas are in each group.

Estimate

Put the Coquinas in a clear container and see if observers can guess the correct amount.

Where in the sand are the Coquinas?

Place a cluster of Coquinas with other kinds of shells in different groups on the sand. See how many can be spotted by an observer.

Did You Know…?

1. Although Coquinas are so tiny, they have been mighty conquers in keeping the British from taking over Castillo de San Marcos in St. Augustine, FL. Over hundreds of years, the clams accumulated and turned into strong limestone rock used to strengthen the fort and absorb cannonball impacts.

2. Tiny clam shells in Southern Florida are known as Coquinas, originating from a Spanish word.

3. The scientific name for Coquinas is Donax Variabilis.

4. In certain places, where the collection of live Coquinas is permitted and the waters do not contain red tide or other pollution, people collect them and make Coquina soup.

5. In many places the collection of living shell creatures is restricted. Checking with the local Fish and Wildlife Department is important when collecting living and nonliving shells.

SOURCES

Florida Fish and Wildlife Commission. *Colorful Creatures in the Beach Community*. http://myfwc.com/research/saltwater/mollusc/other-molluscs/coquina-clams/ Retrieved March 1, 2018

Leal, J. H. (2015, September 18). *The Variable Coquina.* http://www.shellmuseum.org Retrieved March 1, 2018.

Martin, A. J. (2012, March 4). Coquina Clams, Listening to, and Riding the Waves [Life Traces of the Georgia Coast]. Retrieved March 1, 2018 from http://www.georgialifetraces.com

National Park Service. *Coquina - The Rock that Saved St Augustine.* https://www.nps.gov/casa/learn/historyculture/coquina-the-rock-that-saved-st-augustine.htm, Retrieved March 1, 2018.

For more information visit about "Fun with Coquinas" www.writesvillepublishing.com

Tiny clam shells can be found on many beaches around the world. They have different names depending upon their location.

Coquina Beach on Anna Marie Island, in Manatee County, Florida is one place dedicated to the name of these amazing creatures.

There is also a Coquina Beach in North Carolina named after these clams.

Do some research and find out how many other places in the United States are also named after Coquinas.

Glossary

Algae - a simple plant at the bottom of the food chain that can be very tiny for the human eye to see or larger like the size of seaweed.

Bivalve - an animal with a soft body living inside two protective shells hinged together.

Migrate - move to a different place.

Mollusks - a soft bodied animal that does not have a skeletal backbone.

Nutrients - a food source that sustains and promotes growth.

My Coquina Journal

_____

_____

_____

_____

_____

_____

_____

_____

_____

_____

_____

BY_____

ABOUT THE AUTHOR

Laura Pastuszek lives in Sarasota, Florida, holds a BSEd in Elementary Education, with a minor in art, and an MA. She has a lifelong passion for learning, growing, and teaching. Whether as a volunteer, or as a general and special educator, in various settings, she has taught all grade levels including college writing. A love for people and other cultures has taken her to twenty-one countries for personal enrichment and humanitarian purposes. Driven by a great appreciation and curiosity for the beautiful nature, diversity and freedom of the United States, she has been to every state. She started writing poems and her thoughts about life in her journals at the age of nine.